UNCOMFORTABLE
WORDS

UNCOMFORTABLE WORDS

by

JOOST DE BLANK

Archbishop of Cape Town

WITH A FOREWORD
BY THE BISHOP OF LONDON

LONGMANS, GREEN AND CO
LONDON ★ NEW YORK ★ TORONTO

LONGMANS, GREEN AND CO LTD
6 & 7 CLIFFORD STREET LONDON W I
THIBAULT HOUSE THIBAULT SQUARE CAPE TOWN
605–611 LONSDALE STREET MELBOURNE C I

LONGMANS, GREEN AND CO INC
55 FIFTH AVENUE NEW YORK 3

LONGMANS, GREEN & CO
20 CRANFIELD ROAD TORONTO 16

ORIENT LONGMANS PRIVATE LTD
CALCUTTA BOMBAY MADRAS
DELHI HYDERABAD DACCA

First published 1958

PRINTED IN GREAT BRITAIN AT
THE BOWERING PRESS, PLYMOUTH

CONTENTS

FOREWORD

HERE is a very welcome legacy to London from the Archbishop of Cape Town, and not to London only, for his book will, I have no doubt, be read in all parts of the world. We in London owe him a great debt of gratitude for all he has done for us in many fields and now an ever larger number of people will thank him for his words. I am sure this Lent Book for 1958 will find its way into a great many homes and, I hope, hearts and minds.

✠ HENRY LONDIN:

CHAPTER ONE

UNCOMFORTABLE WORDS

Our Lord's 'comfortable words' are familiar to most English communicants. There are traditionalists who do not much care for them because they were not included in the Church's ancient liturgies, and they like to regard them as a modern interpolation dating from the Reformation. But even so three centuries of constant usage have won for them a warm place in many hearts.

In our Prayer Books, after the Invitation and the Confession, come the words of Absolution bringing the assurance of God's forgiveness to the humble penitent; and then to make assurance doubly sure the celebrant says: 'Hear what comfortable words our Saviour Christ saith unto all that truly turn to him'. He reminds the worshippers of two of our Lord's promises—'Come unto me all that travail and are heavy laden, and I will refresh you' (St. Matthew 11:28), and, 'So God loved the world, that he gave his only-begotten Son, to the end that all that believe in him should not perish, but have everlasting life' (St. John 3:16). Then these are followed by two more scriptural quotations, one from St. Paul and the other from St. John: 'This is a true saying and worthy of all men to be received, That Christ Jesus came into the world to save sinners' (1 Timothy 1:15), and, 'If any man sin, we have an Advocate with the Father, Jesus Christ the righteous; and he is the propitiation for our sins' (1 John 2:1).

These words have brought encouragement to countless worshippers, even though it is well known that with the passage of the centuries the word 'comfortable' has changed its meaning. When it was first used in our post-Reformation Prayer Book, it still meant 'strengthening' or 'reinforcing'. Now we think of it much more as bringing consolation, as lightening the burden that a man has to carry. The quality of the word has changed from the active to the passive—not so much encouraging to action as helping to accept.

But even in this modern sense we cherish the 'comfortable words'. Life is often difficult and it is wonderful to hear these promises of sympathy and understanding. A religion that thus enables us to endure life's sorrows and hardships grows increasingly precious. We are quite aware that we ought to think of the words in more vigorous terms, that they ought to incite us to action more than they do, but the mere promise of comfort is often good enough for us.

It is as the antithesis to the meaning we usually attribute to the 'comfortable words' that this book has been given the title *Uncomfortable Words*. As well as *comfortable* we need to 'hear what *uncomfortable words* our Lord Jesus Christ saith'—because this is the season of Lent when we think less of the solace of our religion and more of its demands, when we think less of what it can do for us and more of what *we* can do.

There are plenty of uncomfortable words to

choose from, and they are not so unlike the
comfortable ones as we at first suppose. For
even the comfortable words we cherish have
a sting in their tail lest we too readily take
our ease in Zion. The invitation, 'Come unto
me', is quickly succeeded by the call, 'Take
my yoke upon you and learn of me, for I
am meek and lowly in heart.' It may appear
simple enough to come; it is certainly not
simple to learn the way of meekness and low-
liness. There is a guarantee of discomfort
along that route. Again, the gracious promise
that 'God so loved' is in its turn followed by
the warning that 'he that believeth on him
is not condemned but he that believeth not
is condemned already'. Spiritual choice and
moral decision are always required.

In the pages that follow we have chosen
some of the words of challenge with which
our Lord confronted His disciples. The purpose of this book is to help us to keep our
Lent more faithfully by a straightforward consideration of these selected uncomfortable
words. They are just as important as the

comfortable ones and they should not be neglected.

It ought perhaps to be added that this book is devotional in intent, not expository or exegetical. There are many Scriptural sayings attributed to our Lord which are hard to explain: our object is not to interpret these in order that we may the better understand them (valuable as such a book might be), but to look afresh at some of His familiar sayings that we may be shaken out of our complacency and yield our lives more completely in His service.

I pray therefore that this book will assist us to a good Lent, not so much in spite of, as because of the demands made upon us. And should we feel at all discouraged we can take heart from the fact that we are in good company. The writer to the Hebrews enjoins us to look to Jesus 'who for the joy that was set before him endured the Cross despising the shame'. The servant is not greater than his Master, and the best servant is like his Master. Our Saviour Christ said no uncomfortable words to others which He did not in full measure apply to Himself. He Himself had to come to His Easter by the way of the Cross.

If we follow His directions faithfully we shall always find Him at our side.

CHAPTER TWO

PERSONAL DENIAL

If any man will come after me, let him deny himself, and take up his cross daily, and follow me.
St. Luke 9:23

THIS is where we expect Lent to begin. The call is to deny ourselves, to take up the Cross, to take it up daily, and to follow Christ. The trouble with a word like 'self-denial' is that it has taken on an almost professional meaning. We use it to refer to little pleasures and habits not really sinful in themselves but which we shall be better without—at least for a season. Cigarettes and sugar, cream cakes and sweets, these are the items of our decisions as Lent begins. We have a bit of a struggle on Shrove Tuesday about what to give up, but once we have made up our minds we are rather pleased with ourselves and we feel that we are taking the season of Lent seriously.

7

But there is no virtue in a self-denial that singles out a few details of our lives while the rest remains untouched. We may be able to fool our consciences for a little while by such means but not for long. Our specific acts of self-denial are of value only in so far as they are sacramental of the self-denial of the whole life. The call of Jesus is not to say 'no' to petty vanities and indulgences but to say 'no' to our *selves*—to say 'no' to the self-government of our lives and to hand the authority over to Him.

This call is far more demanding than at first appears for it is never easy to say 'no' to myself. Our Lord was at pains to emphasize its costliness by describing it as the nailing of the self to the Cross. And once is not enough —not even once a year in Lent. The life of self-negation has to be entered upon anew day after day until the end of time. Last year's decision will not do for this—nor, for that matter, will yesterday's.   But each succeeding day the same self-abdication has to be executed and the vacant throne handed over to Christ's occupancy while the rebellious self is again done to death upon the Cross.

The true Christian is the one who understands the total demand his Lord makes upon his life. The truly converted man is the one who on his own Damascus Road falls on his knees before the Christ and cries: 'Lord, what wilt thou have me to do?'

Again and again in Holy Scripture we are reminded of our Lord's life and death, not only that we may rejoice in His atoning work, but also that we may take Him for our example. Christ suffered for us—leaving us an example that we should follow in His steps (1 Peter 2:21). Even Christ pleased not Himself (Romans 15:3). Let this mind be in you which was also in Christ Jesus . . . who humbled Himself and became obedient unto death, even a death on a Cross (Philippians 2:8). And this is the Christ who asks us to share His Cross and calls us to follow Him.

It is high time we rejected our comfortable religion, where all the words are comfortable and where nothing to disquiet us is ever said.

B

It is high time we stopped trying to bribe people to come to church by a variety of entertainments and social recreations. That is to say it is high time we told them quite frankly what Christian discipleship entails, so that for whatever reason they first come they are not left in the dark. They should realize beyond all doubt that there is no Christianity apart from a Cross.

But do we ourselves really know and understand? In colloquial conversation people regularly refer to their unavoidable sufferings as the Cross they have been called upon to bear. Thank God, they are able to use their sufferings and to offer them to God but, strictly speaking, the taking up of the Cross is not an inescapable event but an attitude of life that they have *willingly* adopted for themselves. With us as with our Lord the Cross is always a matter of personal choice.

No one is forced to embark on the life of discipleship but he who does should clearly understand that the disciple is expected to travel the way of the Cross. How ridiculously conventional and comfortable much of our churchgoing appears in the light of Christ's call. We turn up in church if the weather is not too bad (for too bad weather keeps us at home); we turn up if the weather is not too good (for too good weather drives us into the country); we give our alms without pre-meditation and often without sacrifice. We slouch through the services, kneeling lazily, listening sleepily, standing leisurely, with hands in pockets for the Creed and with scant attention to the hymns or prayers.

We are to say 'no' to ourselves. We are to say 'no' daily. We are to hand over our lives to the judgement of the Cross; and we are to follow Christ. For our Lord it meant giving up the job He loved doing. It meant leaving home and being misunderstood by those nearest to Him. It meant a life of uncompromising morality. It meant death by crucifixion —but then, a glorious Resurrection.

By no means are all of us asked to resign our jobs and start a different life, though it happens to a few. But the principle remains the same:

that at work and play, at home and away from
home, the shadow of Christ's Cross is to fall
on all that we are and do—on our expenditure,
on our work, on our leisure hours and hobbies,
on our family loyalties and on all our personal
relationships. Always we are to say 'no' to
self that we may say 'yes' to God.

Do we honestly consider our Lenten self-
denial in such all-embracing terms? Many
years ago now John Watson wrote:

> The Cross is wrought in gold and hung from
> the neck of light-hearted beauty; it is stamped
> on the costly binding of Bibles that go to
> church in carriages; it stands out in bold relief
> on churches that are filled with easy-going
> people. The Cross has been taken out of Jesus'
> hands and smothered with flowers; it has be-
> come what He would have hated, a source of
> graceful ideas and agreeable emotions. When
> Jesus presented the Cross to His disciples He
> was certainly not thinking of a sentiment
> which can disturb no man's life nor redeem
> any man's soul, but of the unsightly beams
> which must be set up in the midst of a man's

pleasure, and the jagged nails which must pierce his soul.

Time has not weakened the impact of these words. Self-denial, which is truly a denial of the self, lifts our Christian faith and practice out of the realm of personal hobbies (where collectors and sparetime craftsmen are prepared to make great and costly sacrifices in order the better to pursue their interests) into the realm of divine power and redemption. It has nothing to do with a negative puritanism that decides quite arbitrarily what is, or is not, legitimate for the Christian to do. In fact, it is little short of tragedy that the average observer honestly believes that the churchman's self-denial is a deliberate attempt to evacuate life of all that gives pleasure and enjoyment. There is many a Christian who feels his conscience is prompting him to renounce some harmless amusement but whose essential self-centredness remains inviolate and unchallenged.

Our Lord was careful to warn the disciples

against those who made an outward show of their fastings. He knew too well that practices thus externalized often confirmed the essential self in its pride and self-sufficiency.

On the other hand we are so good at deceiving ourselves that we may fully intend the total self-surrender our Lord demands without working out its implications in everyday life. For the man who is gluttonous by nature, abstinence in the way of food may indeed be indicative of his honest and deliberate self-denial. But for the man who is avaricious by nature abstinence is no problem—he can take it in his stride. Perhaps for him the reality of his denial would be seen in the size of his contributions to the upkeep of his church and parish. Again, for the man who is lusty by nature it need be no hardship to double or treble his almsgiving, but it would be a very different matter if he controlled his reading to say nothing of his thoughts, his eyes, and his hands.

Our individual self-denying ordinances can never be a substitute for our total self-commitment. But our total self-commitment will almost always express itself in some specific and costly decision. This is clearly portrayed for us in the well-known story of the Rich Young Ruler. Here is a young man with high ideals and religious enthusiasm. He has heard about Jesus, has no doubt often listened to Him as He spoke, has seen Him at work. In Jesus he recognizes the obvious leader of a new moral and spiritual crusade; and in such a crusade he would like to share. When therefore an opportunity comes for a personal conversation he runs to Jesus, falls on his knees, and cries: 'Good Master, what shall I do that I may inherit eternal life?' Our Lord leads him on gently. He unveils his sincerity and enthusiasm; then with unerring diagnosis He lays His finger on the vital spot: 'One thing thou lackest; go thy way, sell whatsoever thou hast, and give to the poor, and thou shalt have treasure in heaven; and come, take up the cross, and follow me.' (St. Mark 10:21)

Some of the saddest words in all Scripture follow this challenge. We read that the young man, now sad and downcast with all passion spent, 'went away sorrowful; for he had great possessions'.

Not all of us are thus called upon to give everything away; only some of us find that our concern and pride of possessions stand between God and ourselves. There are many other roadblocks. It took Augustine a long time to reach the point of conversion, and for him the delay was due to the fact that though he prayed, 'O God make me chaste', he was honest enough to add the words—'but not yet.'

'If any man will come after Me', said Jesus, 'let him say "no" to himself and nail it to the Cross day after day and follow Me.' Nothing could be more demanding, and generally that demand will be focused upon one habit, one practice or one attitude, the abandonment of which will mean an agonizing self-crucifixion. The road to fullness of life is concentrated upon one narrow door through which it will be pain and grief to pass. But we declare ourselves willing, for otherwise we can no longer follow and Jesus will go on without us. No sacrifice is too great if we may walk through life in step with Him.

CHAPTER THREE

FAMILY LOYALTIES

If any man come to me, and hate not his father, and mother, and wife, and children, and brethren, and sisters, yea, and his own life also, he cannot be my disciple.

St. Luke 14:26

A T a first reading we are shocked by these words. Can it be possible that our Lord who was gentleness itself really uttered so shattering a statement? Why—we have always thought of Christianity as the main bulwark of family life. The Church has been prepared to be unpopular in the eyes of the world in its insistence on the sanctity of the marriage bond. It maintains that in marriage man and wife become one flesh and that their union creates a condition which is permanent and indissoluble in this life. It makes much of the Holy Family as the model and example of home life at its best; and it recalls with

18

gratitude that in His dying agony our blessed Lord made provision for His Mother.

But it is precisely the value that our religion sets on family ties that compels our attention to these words. They are the more significant because they were spoken by One who loved His own family, who believed in the family, and who accepted it as a divine institution. Nobody would dare to drive a wedge into the family to separate its members from one another unless there were a higher loyalty to which even family ties must take second place. This higher loyalty Jesus recognized. Man's first allegiance must be to God. It must take precedence over all lesser loyalties. Though of all earthly ties those that bind a family together come first, yet there is a divine loyalty that demands man's primary obedience even at the cost of family unity and solidarity.

In this country, no one is likely to have to choose between God and his family. We are not normally confronted with so forthright and direct a choice. Matters are very different in other parts of the world. If a high caste

Hindu decides to be a Christian, the chances are that his parents will disown him and will deny that he is any longer a member of the family at all. So far as his relations are concerned he will be regarded as dead and gone. And nearer home in Germany and in Russia enthusiastic Nazis or zealous Communists have ostracized those of their families who maintained their Christian faith and practice. Here in Britain we are more tolerant; we allow more generously for the quirks and vagaries of human nature and few will be persecuted for their Christian profession.

But problems in plenty remain. Downright opposition is on the whole easier to deal with than indifference. And the indifference of a family may be a much subtler danger to a person's soul than straightforward hostility. No one minds another's religion so long as it is not too sedulously followed. A respectable Christianity is welcome enough, but what if its demands cease to be conventional? We are right to cherish our homes—and in these troublesome times a peaceful and happy home

may well be our most precious possession—
but its peace and happiness can be bought at
too high a price. For instance, we may have
grown aware of new demands that our Lord is
making upon us. Some of these may be quite
simple, such as a call to go to an early service
every Sunday morning instead of once a
month or once a quarter. But we know that
if we were to translate our conviction into
action we should disturb the well-worn pattern of our Sundays at home; and as we have
no desire to create a disturbance we let it
slide.

I deliberately choose such an apparently
trivial matter to help us to realize how in-
sidious is the temptation to put the family before God. But it can strike home far more
deeply. What happens, for example, if one
member of the family wants to make a sacri-
ficial response to the needs of the Church
overseas while the other partner wants a new
car or refrigerator? And more deeply still:
what happens when the only son instead of
going into his father's business heeds a call to

the sacred ministry and offers himself for ordination?

Rightly and naturally we want our families to be happy families and we want our family relationships to be happy ones. All the same, our Lord warns us that we cannot be His disciples if we conserve that happiness at the price of our convictions, if the family maintains a workable togetherness only by our compromising on our loyalty to God. This is not to say that we have the right to force our convictions upon the rest of the family, asserting that they are God's will for us (and probably for them as well) without discussion and consultation. But when all is said and done God's will must come first.

The truly happy home is a family all of whose members are bound together in a common loyalty to God and to one another. Such a home is made up of people who seek God's will together. Jesus left us in no doubt that there might be times when we should have to choose between family and God, but if the *whole* family is united in a passionate desire to do God's will such a choice need but seldom be made. In such devoted homes there should never be the pain and anguish of misunderstanding, though the pain and anguish of separation and sacrifice are an inescapable part of the life of discipleship. The mother who waves 'goodbye' to her only son as he leaves to serve the Church in some remote diocese overseas is naturally torn by grief at the long separation, but her grief is as nothing when compared with that of the mother who waves 'goodbye' and who does not understand, or even want to understand, why her only son is behaving in what is to her so cruel and heartless a manner.

In a united Christian home, where everyone seeks to obey God in all things, the suffering when it comes will be alleviated by a common dedication—an alleviation denied to those families where no such common dedication is known. But the real heartbreak comes when members of a family, though united in their love of God, fail to see eye to eye and one does something that aggrieves the others.

In families where husband and wife pray *together* (and not only separately), where parents pray *with* their children (and not only teach them to say their prayers), this misunderstanding is much less likely to arise. Nevertheless it *may* arise; and should such a moment come, we must respect the integrity of the one who makes what to us may be a wrong decision in the conviction that so far as he is concerned and so far as he can discern the divine will, he must obey God rather than man.

Lent is an obvious time for us to examine our family relationships afresh. We naturally tend to assume the conventions and the customs of our social milieu; we find it easy to adopt the current standards of behaviour and morality—and all these are worthy of careful consideration. For if we really wish to be numbered among our Lord's disciples, we must give time to our relations with one another. What of my love, my concern for comfort for those I cherish, my desire for peace, my dislike of change, my eagerness to keep up with the Joneses—have these blunted the sharp edge of my Christian obedience? And what about the challenging alternatives of security and insecurity?

So much is comprehended in our Lord's solemn words. They are a demand to put God first at any cost whatsoever. Nothing may be allowed to stand between His command and our obedience. God's will must come first without any reserve. We are to *hate* father or mother, child or parent, yes—life itself, lest any of these should deflect us by one hair's breadth from our total commitment to God. We are shocked by the use of the word *hate*, but our Lord is determined to leave us in no doubt that anything or anyone that comes between the disciple and his obedience to God deserves our hatred. A work of art may be a beautiful thing in itself but if it is worshipped as an idol it is a thing to be hated and rejected. The strength of the language is an indication of the importance of putting first things first whatever the cost or the consequences.

c

The dearest idol I have known,
Whate'er that idol be,
Help me to tear it from Thy throne
And worship only Thee.

Our being instructed to *hate* our dear ones is a matter of the will and not a matter of feeling or emotion. We know that our Lord understood and underlined the importance of family love. But so far as the direction of our wills is concerned, nothing and no one—nothing at all, however precious, no one at all however cherished—may impede our instant obedience to every whisper of the divine will. Only so can we be His disciples.

CHAPTER FOUR

SOCIAL OBLOQUY

*They shall put you out of the synagogues: yea,
the time cometh, that whosoever killeth you will
think that he doeth God service.*

St. John 16:2

IN the Bishop of London's Lent Book for
1957 entitled *Flame in the Mind* its author,
the Reverend Gordon Phillips, tells the story
of Justin Martyr's examination before the
Roman magistrate. Rusticus the magistrate
says to Justin: 'Obey the Gods at once and
submit to the Emperor.' Justin says: 'To
obey the commandments of our Saviour Jesus
Christ is worthy of neither blame nor condemnation.' After further examination Rusticus challenges him: 'Are you not then a
Christian?' Justin replies, 'Yes, I am a
Christian.' And on this unequivocal admission
Rusticus pronounces sentence: 'Let those
who have refused to sacrifice to the gods and

to submit to the imperial commands be beaten, and led away to be beheaded, according to the law.' So Justin died.

It seemed to the authorities so small a thing to ask the Christians to do. Rome was very sympathetic towards all sorts of religions, and there was room for any number of gods in its pantheon. Why, then, be so stupid as to refuse to burn incense to the Emperor and to acknowledge his divinity? It need not spoil anybody's private faith, and, after all, everyone knew that this Emperor-worship was much more a political move than a religious one. But should the Christians insist on maintaining their intransigence only one course was left open to the authorities: law and order must be preserved at all costs and, therefore, those who broke the law must undergo its penalties. 'How maddening these Christians are', said the Romans to one another, 'such good people, but so desperately narrow minded!'

People still say the same to-day: 'Such good people, but so desperately narrow-minded', when it comes to divorce or doubtful outgoings listed on the expenses sheet or anything of that nature. We like a baptism by sprinkling in our national and community life. Religion gives an air of respectability to many of our institutions. For instance, Parliament begins its work with prayers and so do many local borough meetings. It is advisable to ask God's blessing on our man-made plans. We can ask His blessing while making certain He is given no chance to interfere. But baptism by immersion—this is quite a different matter. This means not just a pious hope for the divine approval but a frank submission to the will of God. It calls for a determined effort, first to discern God's will, and then to do it. And this makes life far too uncomfortable for the non-Christian. Christians who compromise are all right, but—from the average person's point of view—the uncompromising Christian is a menace!

Yet this should occasion us no surprise. Did not Jesus Himself say: 'If the world hate you, know that it hated me before it hated you.

If ye were of the world, the world would love its own; but because ye are not of the world, but I chose you out of the world, therefore the world hateth you'?

There is a sense in which this nation can still be called a Christian country. Much of its legislation, particularly in regard to social services and social welfare, has had its origin in the pioneer work and prayers of Christians. There has been a genuine attempt to honour God's laws—or most of them—and on the whole the people would be grieved to lose their parish churches. In general, the State is prepared to acknowledge its debt to the Church and to the inspiration of its teaching. But sooner or later the conflict comes. It may be postponed, it may be staved off by concession and compromise on both sides, but one day the Church awakens to find that the battle has been joined. In its willingness to render unto Caesar the things that are Caesar's the Church has sometimes been dangerously near to rendering to Caesar the things that are God's. There are not a few who would main-

tain that this in fact the Church has done too
often in its history. Be that as it may, it has
only rarely been a deliberate betrayal; and
generally the Church has called a halt to any
further accommodation when its fundamental
obedience to God has been called in question.

The world frequently fails to understand
the Church's attitude. It has such a naïve idea
of what Christianity is all about. Dr. Goebbels,
for example, was quite prepared to give per-
mission for the Church to go on doing, as he
thought, its proper job—that of preparing
human souls for the life hereafter—but he
refused to allow the Church to interfere in
man's social life and material existence. But
the Christian faith is not an other-worldly
religion in the sense Goebbels believed. It *is*
other-worldly, but it does not see an un-
bridgeable gulf between this world and the
next, the two going on independently of each
other. On the contrary, because of the Incarnation the other world has invaded this
present world; and the story of Christianity
is the increasing penetration of this world of

flux and change by the world of Christ's eternal Kingdom. The Christian is therefore a citizen of two worlds, and so far as in him lies he tries to be loyal to both his allegiances. But when the day dawns on which he cannot reconcile his twofold allegiance he has to assert with the apostles in The Acts that 'we have to obey God rather than man'. His is our primary loyalty and, should there be the necessity for choice, the Christian elects to serve his God.

This not unnaturally leads at least to unpopularity if not to oppression or persecution. As soon as the Church in Germany raised the standard of revolt against Hitler's neo-paganism hostilities broke out, and in the conflict the State with all its material power seemed an easy winner. It could imprison the Church's leaders and forbid Christian instruction; it could threaten severe penalties to all who tried to live by Christian standards in opposition to the State's official ruthlessness; it could claim the imminent extinction of the Church, as other tyrants had done in days gone by. But as always, the blood of the martyrs is the seed of the Church. To-day the Church in Germany has found new strength and relevance while Hitler's name and all he stood for is obsecrated and condemned.

The German Church, predominantly, Lutheran, did its best to avoid interfering in the affairs of the State—but the moment came when it had to withstand the devilish machinations of the Nazis, and its persecution followed. Germany is an obvious example of the conflict that can arise between this world and God's world. And it will be with us till the end of time. It happens at all levels —not only on the national but on the local and party levels also. The loyalty a man has for the association to which he belongs is so admirable a quality that nobody wants to interfere with it. We feel like honouring the man who pledges his allegiance in such terms as 'my country, right or wrong'. It reminds us of the mutual marriage vow when husband and wife take each other not only for better but also for worse, for poorer as well as for richer.

But this is to confuse loyalty with identification. Loyalty does not mean an agreement based on an absence of principles or standards. Many a man has chosen to identify himself with his country or his party in dark and difficult days, even when these difficulties are the direct consequence of policies against which he has fought. Nevertheless, as a Christian his primary loyalty must be to God. If his temporal conflicts with his spiritual loyalty, the latter must come first. For this reason there were good men, both good Christians and patriotic Germans, who in the last war could only hope and pray for the defeat of their own fatherland. They could see no other means of bringing their own beloved country to its senses.

It is hardly surprising that the authorities bitterly opposed such action and attacked religion with all the forces at their disposal. Secular totalitarianism and the Christian faith can never walk hand in hand for long.

But this attitude is not limited to illiberal leaders and dictators. When William Temple attempted to bring peace into the industrial disputes of the 1920s, Stanley Baldwin, the Prime Minister, was highly indignant. His dislike of this meddlesome bishop was not so very different from Henry II's cry concerning St. Thomas Becket—'Who will rid me of this turbulent priest?' Not that Baldwin advocated such extreme treatment! But he declared angrily that such interference was as ill-timed and uncalled for as if he himself should attempt to rewrite the Athanasian Creed.

The Christian who tries to be obedient to his Lord is certain to be shot at from two sides. He will expect to be attacked by his non-Christian contemporaries, and he can make some sort of provision for their hostility. But he may not be expecting what can be a far more savage assault from those he deemed to be his religious friends and allies. But, alas, there are any number of religious folk who wish nothing so much as to cultivate their own souls in peace, and who are frightened by those who carry their religion into the market-places and council chambers of the world. They feel, not without reason, that their hot-headed fellow-believers will so strain the world's patience as to bring retribution upon all their heads. Hence, they will urge the complete separation of religion from political action in any form whatever and they will maintain that there is no possible connexion between them.

But theirs is an unrealistic attitude. Living as he does in a collective age, modern man's individual actions and judgements are all the time being conditioned and coloured by the groupings to which he belongs. To strike or not to strike, to ostracize a rebel, to insist on an honest tax declaration, to take a stand on the permanence of the marriage bond, to demand a high standard of public morality—these are matters about which decisions have daily to be taken. And there is not the slightest doubt that there will be occasions when the Christian by virtue of his Christian obedience will be the odd man out. He cannot ignore such issues; nor can he pretend that they have nothing to do with his discipleship. He has to come down on one side or the other, basing his decision on what he considers Christian principles. And if he is in a minority of one, not only he but the whole Church will be condemned for his obscurantist or reactionary convictions.

If we have never been faced with this kind of choice we ought to look again at our Christian profession and loyalty. The issue is not always one of great moment. It may be a tit-bit of malicious but unproven gossip at an afternoon tea-party or a smoking-room story suggestively recounted after dinner—but it develops into far bigger issues. If the world found cause to hate our sinless and all-perfect Master, it will far more easily and readily find cause to hate us.

No faithful Christian can pass through life without enduring social obloquy from time to time. When Jesus told His disciples that the hour would come when those who killed the disciples would think they were doing God service, He went on to say: 'And these things will they do unto you because they have not

known the Father nor me.' (St. John 16:3)
The world will never object to a non-incar-
national religion. But in the Word-made-
Flesh, God has set His seal upon the whole of
life, material and physical as well as private
and spiritual. The Christian cannot keep his
Christianity in a water-tight compartment,
not allowing it to penetrate his social and
political life. He has to take his faith with him
to his work and wherever he goes. Sooner or
later he will find that he has to choose between God and man. When that day comes for
us, may we have the courage to 'go to Him
without the camp (expelled from the community to which we have always belonged)
bearing His reproach.'

CHAPTER FIVE

STRANGE REWARDS

And when they came that were hired about the eleventh hour, they received every man a penny. But when the first came, they supposed that they should have received more : and they likewise received every man a penny. And when they had received it, they murmured against the goodman of the house . . . but he answered one of them and said, Friend, I do thee no wrong. . . . Is it not lawful for me to do what I will with mine own? Is thine eye evil because I am good? So the last shall be first, and the first last : for many be called, but few chosen.

St. Matthew 20:9-11, 13-15

THE Englishman's insistence on fair dealing is one of his greatest qualities; so much so that the British conception of justice and judicial procedure has been adopted and copied in many parts of the world. We are particularly proud of the incorruptibility of justice in this country. Every man is deemed innocent until he has been proved guilty; the fact that our judiciary stands outside politics, which means that our judges never have to trim their legal sails to suit the prevailing political wind; the provision through our *habeas corpus* acts that no one may be held in prison without being brought to trial—these and many other aspects of our legal processes are matters of which we have a right to boast.

But just because of the exalted position we give to justice we are in two dangers. First, there is the danger of mixing up justice and rights. When a man tells us that he is going to stand on his rights he has already convinced himself that he is demanding justice. But the onlooker is not always so certain. He knows that justice is certainly a matter of rights, but not of rights alone—it is also a matter of obligations, and one cannot be considered apart from the other. The second danger is that of so isolating justice as to make it not only impersonal but inhuman. The most perfect judicial system can never disregard the personal element; man can never be treated as a lifeless object. He is alive, he has a mind and a will, and his environment and upbringing have helped to make him the man he is. The actions he commits cannot be viewed in isolation. They are related both to his character and to his circumstances. The man who steals to get food for his starving children is in a different category from the man who steals to secure luxuries for himself.

This personal element must be borne constantly in mind, and more than ever to-day when a collective age tends to treat human beings as 'the masses' or as so many 'hands'—laying down general rules without much thought of individual application. Cold justice is not enough—it has to be tempered by that acknowledgement of personal considerations which we call mercy. And such a quality is more likely to be found in those administrators of justice who recognize themselves as sinners before almighty God and who know that they themselves stand in need of the divine forgiveness. Never has this been better expressed than in the well-known quotation from the prophet Micah: 'He hath showed thee, O man, what is good; and what doth

D

the Lord require of thee but to do justly, to love mercy, and to walk humbly with thy God?'

But though as Christians we endorse the truth of these words, we find it inordinately hard to put them into daily practice. In the story of the labourers in the vineyard, most of us are inclined to think that the grumblers had a very good case. We feel as they did that they were being unfairly treated. Others were being paid as much for a single hour's work as they were receiving for a full day. This could not possibly be called fair. Nor can it—if you look at the story solely in terms of rights: they had done more work and they were therefore entitled to more pay. But there is more to life than demanding our rights. Moreover, there is no suggestion that the late-comers had been deliberately idle. On the contrary, the story suggests that they were unemployed and hoping for a job. They had been as ready to work throughout the day as those who had been hired earlier, but they had been denied the opportunity. Yet their bellies needed food just as badly; their wives and children needed to be provided for just as the others'. And so the merciful employer gave them all the same wages.

To our sensitive ears this sounds dangerously like communism: 'from every man according to his ability to every man according to his need'. But this axiom has never been put into practice in any communist country nor is it likely to be; and the fact that the communists stole the teaching from Christ is no reason for us to disregard it. This is in truth the quality of living that is demanded of every Christian; and it is no use pretending that it will make us popular in our Trade Union branch meeting or in our local Chamber of Commerce.

Though all this is important, yet we must remember that the story of the labourers in the vineyard comes within a specific context bringing its own direct application to those who are Christians in the Christian fellowship. It was told by way of response to St. Peter's well-nigh incredible question. The disciples had just seen the rich young ruler go

away with head and shoulders bowed in utter
dejection. The price Jesus had demanded was
too high for him to pay, and he departed heavy
of soul. Jesus understood, as none of His
followers understood, the nature of the conflict in the young man's mind. And with a
sigh He turned to them and said: 'How hard
it is for them who have riches to enter into
the Kingdom of God.' At this the irrepressible
Peter could keep silence no longer. It mat-
tered nothing to him that his background was
that of a comparatively impecunious fisher-
man; he was proudly conscious that he had
forsaken his boat and his nets to follow Jesus.
The rich young man had failed to pass the test
whereas he and his fellow disciples had passed
with glowing colours. And so, brimful of self-
satisfaction and preening himself complacently,
he asked: 'Behold, we have forsaken all and
followed Thee; what shall we have therefore?'

What an unbelievable question! Here is a
man setting up a profit and loss account with
God. Here is a man who, conscious of the

special sacrifices he has made, thinks that in consequence he should be specially rewarded. Jesus in fairness has to honour the justice of his plea but, having warned the questioner that 'many that are first shall be last, and the last shall be first', He goes on to tell the story of the labourers in the vineyard, and then— at its conclusion—repeats the warning.

There are at least three important lessons for us to learn. First, we have to realize that there is no room for envy in our lives. The labourers were not complaining that they were underpaid or that their employer had not kept his side of the bargain. No, their only complaint was that others who had worked shorter hours should be equally rewarded. In this connexion, the Gospel according to St. John records an illuminating incident at its close. St. Peter is interested to know what is going to happen to him and to some of the other disciples. Our Lord has told him that one day he must be prepared to face martyrdom—and then St. Peter seeing St. John says to Jesus: 'And Lord, what shall

this man do?' To which question our Lord
replies—'If I will that he tarry till I come,
what is that to thee? Follow thou me.' There
can be no envious comparisons in the Christian
life. Others may be more fortunate than we
are. Others may be rewarded and honoured
for service far less faithfully rendered than
our own. But if ever we are tempted to such
odious comparisons we hear our Lord's
words crying in our ears: 'What is that
to thee? Follow thou me.' Nothing else
matters but that we should follow on to know
the Lord. The kind of recognition other
people may receive does not weaken our
resolve or devotion one iota. All that matters,
our whole aim and ambition, is that our lives
should be well-pleasing to Him. If we think
we are going to be fairly treated as the world
counts fairness, we are far away from the
divine reality and we shall be disgruntled by
the successes of others. Jealousy can have no
place in the Christian life.

The second lesson is that goodness does
not necessarily bring its obvious reward in

this world. Although the Book of Job was writ-
ten well over two thousand years ago, there
are still many people who have not absorbed
its teaching. They feel as the Jews of old felt
that virtue should be rewarded in this life,
that prosperity should be their bed-fellow
and that misfortune should pass them by. It is
a tragic fact that there are regular churchgoers in our own day who still have this
attitude; there are people who are resentful
against God because He did not answer their
prayers in the way they themselves had laid
down.

It is hard to learn that Jesus reverses so
many of our generally accepted standards. It
takes time—and prayer—to acknowledge that
true greatness consists not in wielding power
but in washing the disciples' feet. At one
time or another we have all been tempted to
ask the question St. Peter asked: 'What shall
we have therefore?' And in contrast it is perhaps worth remembering a singularly appro-
priate saying from a different context: the
day on which Jesus told His disciples plainly

that no service they could render could be anything like a worthy return for His own self-giving. So far as we are concerned, when we have done all of which we are capable we have only done our meagre duty and we are still unprofitable servants.

The return we can make for the boundless, redeeming love of God is so infinitesimal that we have no rights. His rewards are always out of all proportion to our deserving. And we have to admit that some of us take a very long time to learn that there is no greater reward open to man than the privilege of being allowed to share Christ's Cross.

The third lesson is perhaps the most important—to thank God continually that we are not treated according to our deserts. St. Peter's question shocks us because it demands rewards where we have no right even to expect mercy. Jesus closes this parable with the significant words: 'Many are called but few are chosen.' God's call goes out to everyone but only those who are conscious of their sin and who experience His forgiveness respond,

and in responding discover the wonders of
His grace. There is only one standard in
God's service—not how much we can get but
how much we can give. Those who think of
their religion in terms of success and rewards
have not begun to understand what Christianity is all about. The only measure that has
validity in the Kingdom of God is that of love.
To him or to her that loves much, much is
forgiven—and in the relationship of friendship and love is all the recompense a sinner
seeks. St. Paul learnt this lesson for himself
and passes it on to us in these deathless words:
'I count all things but loss for the excellency
of the knowledge of Christ Jesus my Lord for
whom I have suffered the loss of all things
and do count them but dung that I may win
Christ. . . .' The self-satisfied and envious
labourers could never have understood this
utter self-abandonment. Can we?

CHAPTER SIX

TRUE GREATNESS

*Whosoever will be great among you, let him be
your minister: and whosoever will be chief among
you, let him be your servant: even as the Son of
Man came not to be ministered unto, but to
minister, and to give his life a ransom for many.*
St. Matthew 20:26-8

SOME of our Lord's uncomfortable words
are hard to understand. But there is nothing difficult about the meaning of this
definition of greatness though there is nothing
more difficult than its application. We cannot
get round it or evade its challenge because
placarded before our very eyes is the Son of
Man's own life of service. He was always at
everybody's beck and call. No cry for help
but He responded, even though He had been
on His feet all day and was surely now entitled
to some privacy and rest. Day in, day out, He
lived the truth of His own words that He
had come not to be ministered unto but to

minister, to serve others but not to be served.

That there might never be any doubt in the hearts of His followers, He expressed in pictorial symbolism on Maundy Thursday the attitude of mind which is ever to characterize those who are called by His name. 'Jesus knowing that . . . he was come from God, and went to God; he riseth from supper, and laid aside his garments; and took a towel, and girded himself. After that he poureth water into a bason, and began to wash the disciples' feet. . . . So after he had washed their feet, and had taken his garments, and was set down again, he said unto them, Know ye what I have done to you? Ye call me Master and Lord: and ye say well; for so I am. If I then, your Lord and Master, have washed your feet; ye also ought to wash one another's feet.' (St. John 13: 3-5, 12-14)

It is at the moment when our Lord is most conscious of His divine Sonship, when He is fully aware that He has come from God and goes to God—it is at this moment of unclouded clarity that He reveals the true nature of His authority by Himself gladly engaging in the duties of the meanest house-slave. And so eager is He that we should be left in no uncertainty, He turns to His disciples and says to them plainly and unequivocally: 'Ye also ought to wash one another's feet.'

The Church in England may well have lost something of incalculable value by omitting this action from her rites and ceremonies, except as practised by the reigning Sovereign in a sadly truncated form on Maundy Thursday. All of us who are communicants can never be grateful enough that the Church heeded our Lord's command at the Last Supper to 'do this in remembrance of Me.' How much might the contamination by the world's ideas of rank and greatness have been avoided had the Church been as sedulous in maintaining the practice of washing one another's feet.

This then is to be the pattern of our lives: greatness is to be measured in terms of service, and the greatest of all is servant of all. But such a reversal of the world's standards will never be easy, particularly as the Christian has the difficulty of moving in two realms at one and the same moment. As an ordinary citizen in this world of space and time, he cannot but accept the conventional trappings of rank unless he is called to contract out completely by retiring into a monastery or a hermit's cell. But as a citizen of heaven, greatness is measured solely by humble service—and the two do not go easily together. This is brought home to us in the organized life of that body which is simultaneously temporal and eternal, namely the Church. It has an institutional life in this world, and it has a divine life in the eternal world. In this world it is regarded in much the same light as any other human association; and in its negotiations with Caesar, the methods of Caesar—in so far as they do not encroach upon God's prerogative —have to be adopted. Yet it is a well-nigh insoluble problem to determine how far it is legitimate for the Church to go in its approximation to the customs of the world.

It has tried to find a solution by differentiating carefully between the man and his office.

Not for nothing did some of the saintly medieval bishops wear a hair-shirt next to the skin. It was right that they should accept the dignity proper to their office, but they wanted to remind themselves that their dignity was that of their office alone. Apart from their episcopal status they were one with the humblest penitent seeking absolution—no, even less than the humblest, because from him to whom much had been given would much be required.

Most of us breathe the secular air of the passing world so constantly during our earthly pilgrimage that it is desperately hard to avoid being infected. It is not unknown for an ordained priest to be in danger of thinking of greatness in secular terms, feeling himself somewhat slighted if his work goes on without official recognition. The Archbishop of York in his book *Durham Essays and Addresses* has reminded us that the Church at its best never takes up such an attitude. He quotes these words to his clergy from Bishop Lightfoot's *Ordination Addresses*:

I am ambitious for you all. But my ambition
does not take the form of wishing to see you
in places of emolument or of ease or of comfort or of popularity. I desire above all things
that you should be fit to do Christ's work,
that you should be ready to do it, and that you
should have the scope and opportunity for
doing it. I covet for you not the honour of men,
but the honour of God. If the alternative lay
before me of offering any of you a place of
emolument or dignity on the one hand, or a
place of difficulty and responsibility on the
other, be assured that the emolument and the
dignity should go elsewhere, and the difficulty
and responsibility be laid on your shoulders,
if only I thought them strong enough to bear
the burden.

Yes, the greatest of all is everybody's slave.
Prison visitors tell us that there is no necessity
to add to incarceration, hard labour, discomfort or any additional penalties. The depriva-
tion of liberty is so grievous an affliction that
nothing besides is needed. The house-slave in
the time of our Lord was in the same plight.

He had absolutely no rights. The slightest wish of the least member of his master's household was law for him—not to attempt to obey was quite unthinkable. This is perhaps the hardest of all lessons to learn—that the Christian is never off duty.

His home, where he may feel he has the right to relax, is nearly always the place where the genuineness of his discipleship is most severely put to the test. It is not inordinately difficult to parade our Christianity in the lime-light or in the occasional social encounter; but we feel we have a right to be off our guard at home and, anyway, everybody there knows us so well that it is no use even trying to pull the wool over their eyes. But few would dispute that, in spite of the difficulties, if they honestly make the attempt to adopt our Lord's standards in the family circle, life at home becomes infinitely happier. This new-found happiness makes life in the family far more restful, and its contented atmosphere gives it a strongly recuperative and restorative quality. Those who seek to serve our Lord in the service of others prove in their own experience that His service is perfect freedom.

We find this word of our Lord to be uncomfortable because it is concerned with the little things of life. Most people can screw their courage to the sticking point at some moment of crisis. The hero lies dormant in all of us, and he can be aroused by some sudden disaster or unexpected danger. But there is nothing obviously heroic about this foot-washing business; and even if we might manage it once a year on a Maundy Thursday, this is very different from the house-slave's calendar where the action has to be repeated every day, year in, year out. It is often in the petty things of life that the fiercest battles are fought, and the greatest victories won, for Christ and His Kingdom.

George Morrison in one of his volumes of sermons tells the story of a distinguished Scottish minister who dreamed he had died and gone to heaven. There was St. Peter standing at the gate, and the minister said to him: 'You know, I am the minister who

E

preached to those large congregations Sunday
by Sunday.' St. Peter said sadly, 'We've never
heard of you.' But then he added: 'Are you
by any chance the man who, whatever the
weather, used to go out into his garden every
morning to feed the sparrows?' And when he
replied that he was indeed that man, St. Peter
said with a smile: 'Come in, the Master of the
sparrows wants to thank you.'

Some people, on reading such a story, react
rather angrily by saying that this is sheerest
sentimentalism. But as we grow older we
grow less afraid of this criticism. The man who
has no feelings or who has managed to crush
them or who has convinced himself that every
mood of gentleness is to be dismissed as something soft and unreal is, we find in experience,
not the easiest person to live with. His attack
on sentimentalism is nothing but an attempt
to condone his own continuing selfishness. He
knows nothing of the sympathy of Christ and
he has hardened himself against any possibility
of being moved by another's sorrow or dis-
tress. The sentimentalist—so-called—has been

ostracized in the modern world and 'the tough guy' has taken his place. It would be hard to maintain that humanity generally has profited from the exchange. Besides, the tough guy is a sentimentalist at heart. He is the one type of sentimentalist whose feelings recoil adversely on his own head: he feels pity all right, but it is only self-pity—and there is no more unattractive creature in the world than the man or woman who is sorry only for himself.

Our Lord's sympathy has none of this selfishness about it. His was a complete self-forgetfulness as He shouldered the burdens that others had to bear, in all things enduring their sufferings with them. This He did supremely and uniquely upon the Cross when He chose to take the sins of the whole world upon Himself and in so doing brought salvation to all mankind. The at-one-ment thus wrought was the climax of a life of ministering to others instead of being ministered to—for on the Cross He gave His life to be a ransom for many.

Christianity has been so long in the world

that we forget the novelty of its teaching and take it all for granted. But when Jesus started living like this something new happened. He could therefore say with perfect honesty to His disciples: 'A new commandment I give unto you, that ye love one another; as I have loved you, that ye also love one another.' (St. John 13:34) Something new came into the world with Jesus Christ. It was, however, not so much a matter of teaching but of living. And we who would be true to our Lord and Master and who would obey His new commandment have to learn to put others' needs before our own. The only measure of our service is that we should love others as Christ has loved us. He was actively engaged in redeeming the world, but He had time to look after the needs of those around Him, the crowds in the desert who had grown hungry, the disciples who were over-tired, His Mother in her sorrow as He hung there dying before her eyes.

He was indeed the Suffering Servant of whom the prophet wrote. And we are called upon to love and serve others as He has loved and served us. Which means, quite frankly, that there can be no limit to our self-forgetfulness in the service of others. It is along this road that true greatness is to be found.

CHAPTER SEVEN

THE CRY FOR UNITY

I pray . . . for them also which shall believe on me through their word; that they all may be one; as thou, Father, art in me, and I in thee, that they also may be one in us: that the world may believe that thou hast sent me.

St. John 17: 20, 21

Is this so uncomfortable a word? It comes as a great encouragement to read our Lord's High Priestly prayer in the seventeenth chapter of St. John's Gospel and to discover His continuing concern for us. He prays for His followers and not only those who are alive during His lifetime but those who in future years—and future centuries—shall be numbered among the believers. He prays for them, and therefore He prays for us; and this ministry of prayer continues unceasingly in the heavenlies on our behalf 'seeing He ever liveth to make intercession' for us.

Not only does He pray but He consecrates Himself for our sakes; He reveals to us His glory; He gives us the Word of Life; and He promises us His protection. The provision of the Gospel for all our needs is nowhere more eloquently set forth than in this much read and much loved chapter from St. John, so much so that on marking it attentively the most hesitant Christian finds his timidity turning to strength and his uncertainty to assurance as the realization of God's never failing care comes home to him. Though in prayer to almighty God, our Lord appears to be addressing us directly, and His words of quiet confidence, though spoken to His Father, instil in us the strength that we require.

But there is no question of our basking lazily and pleasantly in the sunshine of God's blessing, for hardly have we felt the warming and soothing power of Christ's concern for us than we are brought up with a start by the words quoted at the head of this chapter. In plain and straightforward language He tells us that the world's faith is dependent on the

Church's unity: 'I pray that they may all be one . . . that the world may believe.'

It is surely more than enough to make us horribly ashamed to realize that our Lord's prayer for unity has for nearly a thousand years remained unanswered. He prayed that all Christians might be united so that their unity might reflect the unity of the blessed and undivided Trinity. That we have failed Him thus far is in truth terrible, but it is not the end of the tragedy. The end of the tragedy is the fact that Christian disunity has been the insurmountable obstacle to world evangelization; and the world does not believe because Christians are not united.

No churchman can sit easily under such a judgement; and every churchman must therefore be deeply concerned about the divisions of Christendom and must work and pray for the healing of its wounds. There are still far too many people who make out that the discussions of possible reunion, the ecumenical movement, the weeks of prayer for unity and similar efforts, are all right for those who like that sort of thing. They imply by their attitude that there may be a handful of enthusiasts who initiate inter-Church conversations and who like going to conferences on Christian unity but that the vast body of Christians, like themselves, want only to be left in peace to continue happily and unmoved in the traditions and practices of their own communions. The awful fact is that they are probably right. Most church folk cannot be bothered—and, in consequence, the world does not believe.

In the West we have lived so long with our various 'churches' that they have become part of the Christian scene and, for the most part, they do not offend our eyes. But the Church overseas has had to face a wholly different situation. The Gospel failed to make its expected impact because of the divisions among the churches. The world *could* not believe while Christians remained in separate compartments. Significantly therefore, the movements of reunion have generally had their origin in what used to be called 'the mission field'. There, the crisis was unavoidable and had to be resolved.

But have we at home the right to be any more complacent? We are only too conscious in these days of the thousands who have no interest in Christianity and who never even consider coming to church. Even in the most vigorous parishes, the church can claim the active allegiance of only a small proportion of the parish population. Of the huge majority, a few will attend church on some family or national occasion, or, perhaps, at Christmas or Harvest; but these are often fitting into a social pattern rather than expressing a religious conviction. No doubt there are additional reasons for this mass indifference but, since we dare not ignore our Lord's own words, we are forced to recognize that our unhappy divisions may well be a major factor to account for this sad state of affairs.

The Christian who would be a faithful disciple must therefore work and pray for the unity of the Church. This will mean in practice that he must take an active interest in efforts that tend towards reunion; and he will work as effectively and intelligently as he can within the context of the ecumenical movement as well as in approaches to the Roman Church. Such participation in no sense calls for a forsaking of principles though it may well call for a forsaking of prejudices—and it certainly demands first of all a thorough knowledge of his own Church and his reasons for being a churchman. It is important, however, that these 'inter-church' contacts should not be left to the theologians and the experts alone but should be maintained by ordinary Christians at all levels, not least that of the ordinary parish and congregation.

Movements of reunion are nearly always in danger of shipwreck not through the wickedness of the instructed but through the stupidity of the ignorant. Nothing is guaranteed to set back the cause of reunion so miserably as those well-meaning Christians who pretend that our divisions are of such minor moment that the best thing is to disregard them in the general acceptance of a lowest common denominator. If the matters which separated the 'churches' were petty and insignificant the divisions of Christendom would be wholly unforgivable and further discussion would be useless. It is precisely because there are serious matters of principle which continue to divide us that there is earnest need for prayer and study, together with a sustained effort for mutual understanding. Not a glossing over of our differences but honest examination is the way back to the unity we have lost. And in such an examination there will be self-criticism as well as criticism of others, there will be confession as well as condemnation. The way to reunion with any 'church' is barred if that church dares to claim its own inerrancy while being quick to condemn the errors of others. Only as we walk in the light as He is in the light can we have fellowship one with another, for only in His light are we all made aware of our own sinfulness from which Christ's redeeming blood alone can cleanse us.

Though the importance of the unity of

Christendom cannot be over-stressed, there is also the importance of the unity of Christians themselves. We must not take this word of the Lord as being applicable only to 'churches', it is equally applicable to people —to me and my neighbour, to me and my family, to me and the other members of my parish church and congregation. It is hard to conceive of any greater disgrace than the assumption on the world's part that church people find it impossible to agree among themselves. 'See how these Christians love one another', may at first have been an honest admission of heathen admiration but in all too short a time it turned into a sneer of cynical sarcasm which has shamed the Christian Church down the centuries. It began very early in the Church's life. Of all St. Paul's letters in none is he more delighted with the believers than with the Church at Philippi. Everything is wonderful: there are no heresies, no blatant sinning, no heated rivalries. It is an idyllic picture of the Church at its best save only for one thing—two women, Euodia and

Syntyche, are always quarrelling and cannot see eye to eye about anything. And so the picture is spoiled because the unity of the Church has been broken. What an unwelcome immortality—to be perpetually remembered and their names permanently recorded as two women who could not get on with each other.

Our Lord's prayer that all those who come to believe in Him may be one is not answered if different types, different ages, different authorities and different sexes have worked out a *modus vivendi* so that they are not at each other's throats. The oneness at the heart of Christianity is not achieved merely by the absence of discord. It is not just a negative quality but something gloriously positive; it is a unity which by bringing unlike things (or people) together creates a richer totality greater in sum than a simple addition of the various items in isolation.

It can be maintained that when St. Paul talks about 'the fellowship of the Holy Spirit' he is referring to the Church, the body of

Christ in which the members find a unity of completion under their divine Head. They are individually fuller personalities because of their union with other believers. The Holy Spirit enriches everyone who finds himself within this spiritual fellowship, and therefore the faithful churchman is more completely developed as a person than if he had not experienced this God-given unity.

St. Paul makes a special point of this in his Epistle to the Ephesians. Here his theme is supremely the summing up of all things in Christ and, in particular, the unity in Christ of Jew and Gentile. He writes: 'He is our peace, who hath made both one, and hath broken down the middle wall of partition between us . . . for to make in himself of twain one new man. . . . Now therefore ye are no more strangers and foreigners, but . . . are built upon the foundation of the apostles and prophets, Jesus Christ himself being the chief corner-stone; in whom . . . ye also are builded together for an habitation of God through the Spirit.' (Ephesians 2: 14 *et seq.*)

Through their unity in Christ, both Jew and Gentile are infinitely richer than they could be on their own, for only as they are 'builded together' can they serve as 'an habitation of God through the Spirit'.

A unity greater than the sum of those constituting it is also recognized in Holy Matrimony, which is but one more example of the positive value set on an acceptance of human one-ness under one God and Father of all. It is tragic therefore that some congregations will condemn such obvious sins as lust and avarice but leave unchallenged the spirit of disruption. How easy it is for us to pass judgement on those sins to which we ourselves are not inclined while ignoring the fact that a poisonous and malicious tongue, a backbiting and tale-bearing habit, may do infinitely greater harm to the cause of Christ. If the greatest of the Christian virtues be love, then to sin against love is to sin against the Holy Ghost.

We think of relations, of business acquaintances, of former friends and fellow members of our local church. Down the long centuries we hear as plainly as when first uttered our Lord's prayer, 'that they all may be one . . . that the world may believe'. Am I in any way responsible for the fact that millions in the world do not believe? And in so far as the remedy is in my hands, am I not in obedience and charity bound to begin to apply the remedy to-day?

F

CHAPTER EIGHT

NO HARD FEELINGS

If thou bring thy gift to the altar, and there rememberest that thy brother hath ought against thee; Leave there thy gift before the altar, and go thy way; first be reconciled to thy brother, and then come and offer thy gift.

St. Matthew 5:23, 24

THIS is our first quotation from the Sermon on the Mount; at least this is what we call it, though it is much more than a sermon —it is our Lord's Manifesto of the Kingdom. In it Jesus lays down the principles that govern His Kingdom and therefore the principles by which Christians ought to live. Sometimes we are tempted to regard it as a code of ideal behaviour in an unreal world, and we try to convince ourselves that it is not meant to be taken too literally. Thus we seek to evade its challenge. But once we have grown familiar with it, it will not let us go. Like the Hound of Heaven Himself, it pursues us down the arches of the years. Now and again it catches up with us; it forces us to attention and re-consideration. We measure our mediocrity against its absolute standards, and we are driven to our knees as we cry, 'God be merciful to me, a sinner.'

Generally, however, the fact that we know the words and can recite much of the sermon by heart effectively manages to cushion us against the soul-shattering shock of its demands. For this reason we have in the earlier chapters taken our 'uncomfortable words' from other parts of the Gospel. As they are not so well-known, we felt they would come alive for us more quickly and directly. But now, pray God, we are ready to listen with new ears to the old familiar words, and in particular to those used to open this chapter. These have been chosen because they follow on naturally from our consideration of *The Cry for Unity*. We have reminded ourselves of the urgent need for unity. The reason why our prayers go unanswered, why we make no progress in the Christian life, why the evangel is hailed as good news by so few of our contemporaries, may well be traced to our disobedience to the demand for unity at the point of personal action. Until we are in love and charity with our neighbours God cannot use us in His service.

God cannot use us because God cannot hear us. We know that the Gospel is the Gospel of Forgiveness. We know that Christ died for our sins according to the Scriptures. We know that new life begins through the washing away of sin. In other words, we know the starting-point. Unless we get past this starting-point we do not set out at all. The only way past it is by the way of God's forgiveness. All this is elementary albeit fundamental. We think we understand it, and at night before we go to sleep we ask God to forgive us for the sins and failures of the day. Probably we rattle off the Lord's Prayer as well for good measure—until one day our complacency is blown to smithereens as we realize for the first time that there is in this prayer one conditional clause, and only one to underline its crucial significance: 'forgive us our trespasses *as we forgive them that trespass against us*.' This is the price of entry into the Christian life, and there are no complimentary tickets. If we are not prepared to pay it we can pray till we are blue in the face, we can fast to the point of starvation, we can read our Bibles till we can no longer see, we can go to church three times a day—but it will all get us nowhere. The path of fellowship with God is not only by way of the divine forgiveness but by way of our forgiveness too—our forgiveness of those who have wronged us and from whom we are estranged.

Considering how regularly the Lord's Prayer is recited it is incredible how often this is overlooked or disregarded. There are numbers of what we should normally call devout Christians who are meticulous in their obedience to the Church's rules, who are horrified by the so-called sins of the flesh, who are quick to condemn those who fall to temptations to dishonesty or indolence, but whose consciences are quite insensitive to the broken relationships in their own family circle and among their acquaintances, a break-down aggravated by the poison of their tongues or the venom of their letters.

St. John recognized the falsity of such an attitude. He stripped things down to the bare essentials and left us in no doubt of the gravity of the sins against charity. For him, the man who thus transgressed was outlawed from God, and all his religious practices were worth-less and hypocritical. Even more than this, St. John held that a man's fellowship with God could be measured only by the degree of his fellowship with other human beings: 'if a man say, I love God, and hateth his brother, he is a liar: for he that loveth not his brother whom he hath seen, how can he love God whom he hath not seen? And this command-ment have we from Him, That he who loveth God love his brother also.' (1 John 4:20, 21), and again, 'if we love one another, God dwelleth in us' (1 John 4:12).

It is not enough to assent to this in general terms—we need to work it out in all the per-sonal interchanges of daily life. What about those people who have wronged us? So many stupid little things are allowed to break up a united family. Something has been said or done at which we take offence and, instead of obeying the scriptural injunction not to let the sun go down upon our wrath, we brood upon it, we allow it to grow out of all proportion to reality, until the damage thus done is hard to undo. We cease to be rational about it; it has assumed a malignant, demonic life of its own and it blots out that essential relationship which is what really matters.

Lent is a time for putting our relationships right. So let us take time for this urgent activity forthwith. We should not be able to say the Lord's Prayer again without thinking of its conditional clause; therefore let us make sure that when next we say it we pray it in a spirit of sincerity—in faith claiming God's forgiveness because we have in fact forgiven all who have sinned against us.

Such forgiveness to be real means in most instances more than just a change in our mental attitudes. Where two people have been at variance for years a change of spirit in one of them is unlikely to be realized by the other unless he is told. The forgiveness we are called upon to exercise is to be a reflection of the divine forgiveness—not the remission of a penalty but the restoration of a relationship. Our forgiveness must therefore reach out to embrace the offender; we must convince him that the separating barrier has been broken down. Like the prodigal in the story of the Prodigal Son who knew that his father's heart of love beat unceasingly for him, so must those who have wronged us know that we are not patronizingly demanding justice or satisfaction, not even apportioning blame, but that we are ready and eager to create an even richer communion than we experienced before.

It is desperately important to guard against a patronizing spirit. Those who have seen that great film on the life of St. Vincent de Paul entitled 'Monsieur Vincent' will remember a scene in which the dying saint warns one of the novices that there is nothing harder in life than to dispense charity without breeding resentment in the breast of the recipient. This is as true of forgiveness as of charity. Nothing is certain to wreck a relationship even more thoroughly than a condescending 'holier-than-thou' or 'more-charitable-than-thou' attitude on our part. The tiny wrong that I can forgive my brother is infinitesimal compared with the incalculable debt that both he and I owe our heavenly Father. My brother and I are fellow-sinners in need of the divine forgiveness, and I have nothing about which to boast or to be superior. Indeed I am the greater sinner because I have been withholding my pennyworth of forgiveness while claiming the infinite forgiveness of God.

Furthermore, should there be any danger of my being patronizing, I need only turn again to our extract from the Sermon on the Mount: 'if thou bring thy gift to the altar, and there rememberest that thy brother hath ought against thee; Leave there thy gift before the altar, and go thy way; first be reconciled to thy brother, and then come and offer thy gift.' This is not a matter of my forgiving those who have wronged me but of my admitting my sins and shortcomings to those whom I have wronged. Here is no occasion for condescension or conceit but, on the contrary, a humble and penitent acknowledgement of my own failures.

The old proverb cannot be applied in every instance without exception but it is almost always true that 'it takes two to make a quarrel'. The fault is seldom wholly on one side. If I am involved in any broken relationship, it is extremely unlikely that all I shall have to do is to forgive without needing also to ask to be forgiven. But even if any such self-righteousness were justified, our Lord does not bother to suggest that my brother's grievance must be a genuine one. If, whether rightly or wrongly, he *feels* that I have failed him then it is still my duty to try to effect a reconciliation although in this regard my conscience may be as clear as the noonday sun. The fact that there is estrangement strongly suggests that I must bear part of the blame.

We should assure those with whom we have been in disagreement that there are no barriers or barricades left on our side. When we have done everything possible to effect a reconciliation, we can then return with confidence to offer our gift. Even though our attempt at reconciliation may not have been accepted, we now have no resentment but continue the more earnestly in prayer that the day may be hastened when we shall be truly united in Christ.

It would be stupid to suggest that a life of this quality is easy. But it would be even more stupid to suggest that it is unimportant. It would be possible to argue that this 'uncomfortable word' spoken by our Lord Jesus Christ is the one hurdle that cannot be by-passed. Forgiveness lies at the heart of the Gospel. And if the reality of our forgiveness is measured by the spirit of forgiveness that finds expression in our lives, then there is nothing in our lives of greater urgency and moment.

At this holy season of the year we love to

stand by the Cross and to marvel again at the wonder of our redemption: 'God was in Christ reconciling the world unto Himself.' Why should He bother? The world had rebelled against Him, the world had wandered away, the world had offended His holiness and His love. Yet it is God who takes the initiative, it is God who so loves the world that He gives His only-begotten Son. He does not wait for man to act. He does not wait for man to ask for forgiveness, but 'God commendeth his love towards us in that *while we were yet sinners* Christ died for us.' As He goes to His death we hear Him say: 'Father, forgive them for they know not what they do.' In the midst of His agony, even then He does not blame or condemn but tries to find excuse for man's heartless cruelty. Our petty prides and disagreements, our quarrels and enmities, our feuds and conflicts, have no place in His flock. We cannot honestly pray 'Lord, remember me when thou comest into thy Kingdom' unless we are prepared to learn to forgive as He forgave.

CHAPTER NINE

PRAYER THAT COSTS

What, could ye not watch with me one hour?
St. Matthew 26:40

THE climax is at hand. The triumph of
Palm Sunday is behind Him. He has
cleansed the Temple and outraged the Jewish
rulers. He has wept over the City and has
spoken words of judgement. He has washed
the disciples' feet and instituted the Holy
Communion. Judas has gone out to betray
Him for thirty pieces of silver. Claiming no
strength but such as all men can have, He
knows that He is coming to the supreme
testing-point of His life. And to prepare Himself, 'he went forth with his disciples over the
brook Cedron, where was a garden, into the
which he entered, and his disciples' (St.
John 18:1).

This was Gethsemane where He loved to
come and pray. Usually when Jesus wanted to

commune with His Father He slipped away
alone with nothing and no one to disturb
Him or to interrupt. But the night of Maundy
Thursday was different from all other nights.
This was His last chance to save Himself—and
yet He already knew the truth of what later
at Calvary His detractors said about Him:
'He saved others, Himself He cannot save.'
He knew He could accomplish the world's
redemption by no other means than the sacrifice of Himself. The words His enemies used
to jeer at Him in His dying agony are words
which make us love and worship Him all the
more. For us men and for our salvation, He
deliberately trod the *Via Dolorosa* and embraced the Cross.

But what a decision for any man to have to
take. Jesus was in His early thirties, a man in
the prime of life. He knew that He had only
to slip away from Jerusalem, to move among
the country-folk of Judaea and, preferably, of
Galilee to undo all the crafty malice of the
Jewish leaders. He knew that He could win
the allegiance of thousands of decent, simple

people—that then He could march on the capital at the head of a popular rising and throw out those who hated His teaching and who were plotting His death.

In his hymn, so well loved, Watts must have had such a picture of Jesus in mind. He wrote: 'When I survey the wondrous Cross, Where the young Prince of Glory died'—*the young Prince of Glory*. As He went to Gethsemane life's possibilities must have appeared boundless. And yet all this He was called upon to cast away in what might be called a suicidal act of self-sacrifice. Was this the right way, the sensible way? As one who was sane and healthy the young Prince of Glory did not want to die. But what if death were the gateway of life not only for Himself but for all mankind?

We can stand only on the fringe of that Gethsemane battle, but the little we can grasp of it is more than enough to convince us of its intensity. The words of Christ's prayer come down to us through the centuries: 'Father, if it be possible let this cup pass from me. Nevertheless, not my will but thine be done.' This is the conflict between duty and desire raised to the nth degree, for this conflict is in the breast of a Man in whom all humanity is embodied, and in whose struggle all men's struggles are included.

As He entered the Garden the pressure of that moral and spiritual conflict was already mounting, and mounting rapidly. He had spent much of His life in prayer. He had come to Gethsemane before in order to pray. But this is the only recorded occasion when instead of seeking solitude for His prayer He called on His disciples to help Him by watching with Him and praying with Him.

In all the time they had known Him, He had never made such a request. Even now He did not make it of all of them but only of His three most intimate friends. What a wonderful privilege to be selected for so sacred a share in His hour of need! Are we not burning to say that we wish we could be numbered among them, and do we not wish that Jesus would ask us as He asked Peter and

James and John? And if He did, would we not pray as we have never prayed before? It seems easy and obvious to say 'yes' to questions such as these until we remember that in fact Peter and his two friends fell asleep in the midst of our Lord's agony—until we remember that in all Holy Scripture there are no sadder words than those our Lord addressed to them as He turned expectantly to them for their strengthening support: 'What, could ye not watch with me one hour?'

But we are not merely recapturing a bit of age-old history. As Pascal wrote, 'Jesus is in agony until the end of time'. Day after day He is being delivered up to death. And day after day, He looks at us and breathes the same question: 'What, could ye not watch with me one hour?'

Of course, if we want to be known as conventional churchgoers and nothing more, these words need not apply to us and we can evade their uncomfortable challenge. But those who are satisfied with a minimal

G

Christianity are not likely to be reading this book. This is for those who would like to do better than that—those, for example, who are taking their Lent seriously because they want to grow closer to our Lord and live more faithfully in fellowship with Him. This is for those who would like to be numbered with Peter and James and John.

There is another line of approach. Although as a man it was natural for our Lord to seek the support of His friends, yet as a man wholly dedicated to God no thought of self ever intruded in anything He did; and therefore we may well believe that He urged the three disciples to watch with Him not for His sake but for *theirs*. In the event, we know He was able to win His battle without their help for they were asleep; but perhaps a little later they would not have been so quick to forsake Him and to run away if only they had stayed awake to pray.

Peter with his hot, impetuous nature certainly needed the stabilizing strength of prayer. James, so soon to be the first apostle

to die for the Faith, certainly needed to prepare himself for what lay just ahead. John,
chosen to be the most profound interpreter
of the nature and redemptive purpose of God,
certainly needed to spend every available
minute in prayer and meditation. And we—
do we not need to pray? Has the sanctifying
grace of God the Holy Spirit yet begun to con-
trol and direct our wayward natures? When
confronted with the acid test, are we ready
at any cost to choose the way of Christ? Has
our love for our Lord and our understanding
of His purpose grown with the years? Are we
better Christians to-day than we were a year,
five years, or ten years ago? If not, can it be
true that we have never taken this Uncomfortable Word to heart, have never set aside
unhurried time for our prayers?

Our consideration of this particular word
appears to be little more than a series of heart-
searching questions, but these are prompted
by our Lord's prior and most incisive enquiry.
It is interesting to note that both Mark and
Matthew record almost identical words—

both of them make a point of mentioning the period of *one hour*. This cannot be a matter of chance. Our Lord so clearly emphasizes a definite time that we do well to take heed to His admonition.

But for a generation of Christians who have been brought up to mumble a few prayers at their bedsides at night and, if exceptionally well-instructed, also to make an act of recollection when they wake up in the morning, the idea of spending sixty minutes in prayer is beyond all reason. They find it hard enough to avoid distractions in the short minutes to which they have accustomed themselves—but an hour would be out of all proportion; and they cannot imagine how they would fill the time.

It is perhaps not so important at first to decide on sixty minutes as to decide resolutely that there shall be a specific period set apart day by day. If we are frightened by the thought of a whole hour devoted to prayer, let us begin with half-an-hour or even fifteen minutes—but, however long or short, let this time be given absolute priority in our lives. This is an appointment that we shall never fail to keep. This comes before our meals, our sleep, our daily chores. It is to be built into the timetable of our normal lives—which means, among other things, that normally the same period of the day will be held inviolate for our private communion with our Lord. If only we can hold to our resolve for a few weeks the habit will have been formed and we shall be as unlikely to give up our prayers as to forgo our meals.

There will be days when prayer will come easily to us, there will be days when praying is the last thing we shall feel like doing—but prayer is not primarily a question of the emotions but of the will. We put ourselves unreservedly at God's disposal, and if He cares to encourage us by granting us a sense of His presence, well and good. But the value of our prayers is not determined by such feelings: in fact, the discipline of holding on in faith when the heavens are as brass may reap a far richer though less obvious reward.

The importance of this specific period in our daily living lies first in the adjustment of our routine that we may give God our unhurried and humble attention. The world with all its demands is so much with us that it is an urgent requirement to hold ourselves deliberately in God's presence day by day. Thus we shall be helped to look at life in proper perspective, in its true colours and not through self-tinted spectacles.

Yet, granted all this, many still draw back because they are honestly scared at the thought of what they would do with the time at their disposal. Let us start by being perfectly natural. The Christian life is a life of friendship with God, and all that makes up our lives is therefore of interest to Him. We begin by sharing our lives with Him, our hopes and fears, our successes and failures, our ambitions and disappointments. We remember that what is of concern to us is, by virtue of our friendship, of concern also to Him; therefore we pray for our families and friends, our parish church with its priests and people, and for the family of God throughout the world. We know how He loved to minister to the poor and helpless, and we shall find that our time is soon gone when we start to pray for those in need.

There is no necessity to be too formal. If we find it hard to kneel all the time, there is everything to be said for changing our position occasionally, for standing up, for walking about, even for sitting down. If we find it hard to begin, there are books of prayers and devotion to help us. There is always the Bible in which we ought to be far better versed than we usually are and of which we ought to read at least a little every day.

There is, too, the need to remember that prayer is a two-way business. Let us not be too eager to fill every available moment with our words, but let us give time for God to speak in the quietness of our souls.

If once we begin to pray like this we shall find that the fifteen minutes which first we allotted are much too short; soon the period will be lengthened to thirty minutes, and then to the full hour—not necessarily all at a stretch but split up as suits us best in the waking hours of the day.

We ought not to rest easily satisfied with any period shorter than an hour. Most of the masters of the spiritual life have underlined the value of this length of time. This is as true of St. Francis de Sales, who wrote his treatise on the life of devotion for those who lived in the world, as of those teachers who wrote for priests and for those in religious orders. We pray that we may never be the occasion of our Lord's lament in Gethsemane: 'What, could ye not watch with me one hour?'

CHAPTER TEN

SO SEND I YOU

As my Father hath sent me, even so send I you.
                                         St. John 20:21

Now the sufferings are over and the Cross is behind us. In the glory of the Resurrection we can forget the rigours of Lent and rejoice in the triumph of Easter Day. This is a time for thanksgiving, a season no longer of mortification but of feasting.

True as this is, it is by no means the whole story. No one wants in any way to minimize the joys of Easter, but we must always remember that our Lord did not leave His scars behind Him in the tomb. They were a sign of recognition. He rose from the dead bearing the marks of His sacred wounds. And when He ascended into Heaven He took His glorified humanity with Him, and in His body were the prints of the nails, the thorns and the spear.

Those dear tokens of His Passion
Still His dazzling Body bears;
Cause of endless exultation
To His ransomed worshippers.
With what rapture
Gaze we on those glorious scars.

Not even in the happiest moments of the Church's year can the Cross be forgotten. Not even on the first Easter Day. 'Then the same day at evening, being the first day of the week, when the doors were shut where the disciples were assembled for fear of the Jews, came Jesus, and stood in the midst, and saith unto them, Peace be unto you. And when he had so said, he shewed unto them his hands and his side. Then were the disciples glad, when they saw the Lord. Then said Jesus to them again, Peace be unto you: as my Father hath sent me, even so send I you. And when he had said this, he breathed on them, and saith unto them, Receive ye the Holy Ghost: whose soever sins ye remit, they are remitted unto them; and whose soever sins ye retain, they are retained.' (St. John 20:19-23)

We can sense the dramatic change of atmosphere. The disciples, confused and fearful, are assembled in the Upper Room. Then, in the midst of their bewilderment, they suddenly realize that they are no longer on their own. Their beloved Master is back with them again. They recognize His voice as He gives them the accustomed greeting. And if there are any doubts remaining, they are altogether dispelled as He shows them the scars of His crucifixion agony. St. John states distinctly the change that came over them, and we can read the wonder of that moment in his simple sentence: 'Then were the disciples glad when they saw the Lord.'

Glad, as are countless Christians every Easter and—for that matter—every Sunday also; for every Sunday is the Lord's Day, the joyous memorial of Christ's Resurrection. But life is not yet an unchanging round of Sundays, and we cannot sit down for long to enjoy the Easter victory in peace as there is still so much to be done. Thus, in St. John's account, we again have a sudden change of atmosphere. Now the disciples are recalled to the cruelty of Golgotha. Our Lord speaks once more. He repeats the same words of greeting: 'Peace be unto you.' First He had spoken to reassure them as their friend; now He speaks to commission them as their Lord and Master. They have just seen the marks of His Passion in His hands and His side; and quietly He says to them: 'As the Father hath sent me, even so send I you.'

He has not come back from the dead that they may be spared His pain and suffering. He has come back to show them that God has more than vindicated His mission and His obedience. He has come back to show them His irresistible power against sin, the world and the devil. And He has come back to call them to a life of commitment as whole-hearted and entire as His own.

His call still sounds in our ears. We bring to mind some earlier words recorded by the Fourth Evangelist. He describes the purpose of our Lord's coming thus: 'For God so loved the world that he gave his only-begotten Son that whosoever believeth in him should not perish but have everlasting life.' And he goes on: 'For God sent not his Son into the world to condemn the world; but that the world through him might be saved.'

God sent His Son into the world not to condemn it but to save it. And the Son tells those that love Him: 'As the Father hath sent me, even so send I you.' Which means that we too are sent into the world not to condemn it but to save it.

We have to admit that on the whole the Church has been better at condemning than at saving. It still is. There are plenty of Church bodies and organizations ready to register their censure or disapproval of this or that social or moral failure, but there are all too few engaged in the work of redemption. The world thinks of the Church as a body of people whose chief function it is to say, 'Don't!' And many men and women are quite convinced that church-people are frustrated 'kill-joys'.

It is of course true that the Church as by

obedience bound has to be fearless in rebuking vice and resisting evil. But if it does no more than this it is not being whole-heartedly obedient, and it is failing to take note of our Lord's words of commissioning: 'As the Father hath sent me, even so send I you.'

We have no doubt that this is an Uncomfortable Word. We find it unconscionably hard to act upon it. Even the keenest of our churchgoers who are eager to serve their parish church in the work of administration and organization, in its services and its worship, in its social and recreational activities—even these are not so quick to come forward when the Church's evangelistic responsibility is under consideration.

There are sensible reasons for this reticence. Most of us have suffered from the-button-holing enthusiast who invades our privacy by demanding, 'Are you saved?' And there is a reserve about the most sacred things of life which is both proper and desirable. Spiritual exhibitionism is a highly unpleasant phenomenon—and we want no part of it. But this does not mean that we reject our obligation to pass on the good news of Jesus Christ.

We do well to remember that our Lord asked us to live our lives as He lived His, not —for most of us—in a literal imitation of its physical circumstances but in the same spirit of selfless service. Our Lord commended the Gospel by what He was and by what He did before commending it by what He said. It is interesting to note how often in the Gospel record these words occur: 'And Jesus *answered* and said . . .'. He began to talk and to explain in response to an enquiry, and that enquiry was usually prompted by some action He had taken.

This is not to suggest that the time never comes when speech is required. Our Lord's words at His Ascension: 'Go ye into all the world and preach the Gospel . . .' are proof enough of this, but the life must preach before the lips. The day will certainly dawn when words will be needed, but as our Lord sent His disciples forth He first reminded them of the wounds in His hands and His side. For us too, the wounds before the words.

He went to the Cross for man's salvation. How much of the Cross is there in our witness? This is the challenge that confronts us to-day; how do we respond? Have we, for instance, ever done so simple a thing as to ask some non-churchgoing friends to come to church with us, and have we called for them and made them feel at home? Have we identified ourselves with any public act of witness in which the Church has been engaged, or has shyness or embarrassment kept us away? How many people at my place of work know that I am a Christian, and—if they know—have I ever tried to pass on the reality of my faith to them? Have we ever offered our services in any evangelistic enterprise in the parish, it may be by visiting or by some other means?

Even if we can say 'yes' to questions such as these, we are still shamed by the smallness of our response as compared with our Lord's self-giving to redeem the world. It may be that much more is asked of us. Christ may be calling some to ordination or the religious life, others perhaps to the service of the

Church overseas. But whether He calls us in this way or not, He most surely calls us to help forward His Church by our prayers, our interest, and our giving. Does the shadow of the Cross fall on our bank accounts and cash books? Unless we make real sacrifices in supporting the Church's missionary work, we fail the challenge.

Every parish and every Christian should spend time to consider our Lord's words—'even so send I you'. There are still far too many people who think of everything to do with church as something planned for their satisfaction and enjoyment. This is all right as far as it goes. Everything to do with the worship of God ought to be satisfying and enjoyable, but the danger is that church membership stops there. As has been said, the only way to keep your Christianity is to give it away. The person who is interested in what he or she gets out of church but is not concerned to pass it on to others has not begun to understand the essence of the Faith.

Those scars in our Lord's Body should be

H

sufficient indication of what is expected of the Church and of all its members. Those who worship a dead Christ may be satisfied to revere His memory withdrawn in an Upper Room, but those who rejoice in a living Christ can be satisfied only by proclaiming the glorious news throughout the world. And to make this proclamation they are prepared to pay the cost.

It will not be easy—but we are not expected to do it by ourselves. When our Lord spoke to His disciples He said: 'As the Father hath sent me, even so send I you'; then, having uttered these words, He breathed on them and said: 'Receive ye the Holy Ghost'. And that promise makes all the difference. His commands are His enablings. He gives no instruction, demands no sacrifice, asks for no action, except in the assurance that He will give us the power to obey. This is as true of all the Uncomfortable Words as of this one. If we are willing, God Himself through His Spirit will work in us, giving us the strength to do His Will.

CHAPTER ELEVEN

FIRST THINGS FIRST

Seek ye first the kingdom of God and his righteousness and all these things shall be added unto you.

St. Matthew 6:33

LENT is over, Easter is here. Our blessed Lord's victory has been consummated; in and through Him we are now to live in the power of His endless life. The surpassing wonder of our most holy Faith is that by our incorporation into the Body of Christ we are joined with Him in His redemptive action. We are buried with Him in Baptism to rise to newness of life. And this new life goes on from strength to strength as we yield ourselves to Him and as we feed on Him in the most comfortable Sacrament of His Body and Blood.

St. Paul could never tire of telling the churches all about this glorious mystery. 'Ye are dead', he wrote, 'and your life is hid with Christ in God' (Colossians 3:3); 'I live yet not I, but Christ liveth in me: and the life which I now live in the flesh I live by the faith of the Son of God, who loved me, and gave Himself for me.' (Galatians 2:20) And as a natural consequence of this divine union: 'If ye then be risen with Christ seek those things which are above where Christ sitteth on the right hand of God.' (Colossians 3:1)

But mystic though he was, St. Paul was nothing if not realist. Although he had no doubt that man's salvation is all of God, equally he had no doubt that man has to strain every nerve to enter into the fulness of that salvation. Only so can man's dignity and free will be conserved. We are not automatic machines. What is ours by faith has to be personally striven for and appropriated. As was once said by St. Ignatius Loyola, the Christian has first to realize that he can do absolutely nothing by himself; he has to accept his own utter helplessness and utter dependence upon God. But then, having reached this point, he has to act as if it all depended upon himself; he resolutely sets his will to put into practice the implications of his discipleship. Not till long afterwards will he understand that the energies he has used in God's service were in fact not his own but God's. He was given the strength to persevere because it was God who was working within him, giving him the will and energy required.

So as we come to the end of our Lenten meditation we are called back to our own personal responsibility. We are risen with Christ—yes—thanks be to God. But as those risen with Christ it is now our duty and privilege to seek those things which are above. It is our obligation to seek *first* the Kingdom of God. The City of God descends to earth out of heaven; and at the same time we have to work with every fibre of our being to hasten its coming.

At the turn of the century Henry Drummond was well known both as a Christian and a scientist not only in his native Scotland but throughout the English-speaking world. He lectured in the university during the week and on Sunday evenings he took Glasgow's largest hall, and there to a packed audience he expounded the Christian Faith. On one memorable occasion he addressed the assembled students on the subject of this uncomfortable saying of our Lord's, and he closed with these words: 'Gentlemen, I beseech you to seek the Kingdom of God first or not at all. I promise you a miserable time if you seek it second.'

There is no doubt that this was good advice, but how hard to put into practice. The business of earning our daily bread, of providing for dependents and of securing the accepted necessities and luxuries of the group to which we belong, is a demanding life. The world is so much with us—it presses on us not only at work but in our leisure too—that it is difficult to recognize that all this must be kept secondary to our quest for the Kingdom.

When it comes to giving to the Church, its work at home or its mission overseas, it is

difficult to make this a first and not a last
charge on our budget. We have grown
accustomed to giving to God a proportion of
what we have left when all other expenses
have been met, whereas our expenses should
be largely determined by what is left after we
have given to God what we believe to be
right.

For many people, church worship is regarded in much the same way. They go to
church if nothing comes along to interrupt
them, but any pleasant interruption consti-
tutes a valid reason for absenting themselves.
They mean to be practising Christians, but
they have never considered their Faith as a
priority in their time-table.

And what of the children? There are some
quite prominent members of church congregations, perhaps serving on the church
council or in some other office, who would
be sadly disappointed if the son decided to
take Holy Orders or the girl to go abroad as a
missionary or to enter the religious life. These
are parents who want, as they believe, the

best for their children, but who have been so contaminated by the spirit of the world that for them the best means *material* well-being. One of the reasons why they spent hundreds of pounds on their children's education was that they should be economically secure; they know that the clergyman is always going to live but a little above the poverty line and therefore they want no part of it for their boy.

It is good to take time to look at our lives—to look at our standards, our programme, the goal we have set ourselves, the conventions by which we live; and in the light of that self-examination to discover whether we are in fact seeking the Kingdom of God first or second or not at all. Henry Drummond was surely right in warning his hearers against putting it second. The out and out materialist, the man who puts all his eggs into this world's basket, has some chance of happiness. He may well live a rounded, integrated life though the level of integration is far lower than that intended for him by God.

But the man who gives lip-service to the

demands of the Christian Faith yet conforms to the standards and predilections of this world is undoubtedly in for a bad time. He will be pulled first in one direction and then in another; at one moment his ideals captivate him, the next he urges the need for realism. These are the people of whom it has been said that they have just enough religion to make them miserable. Their vision of God turns the world's rewards into dust and ashes. But the world's attractions and demands succeed in driving away the vision, which nevertheless constantly returns to haunt them. This for most people is not a deliberate choice or rejection: the world surrounds them all the time and it therefore seems more real and immediate than the Kingdom. They do not mean to seek it second but in fact they do, while lamenting their weakness to themselves.

Much of the trouble is due to our faithlessness. We do not really believe the promise our Lord attaches to this Uncomfortable Word: 'Seek ye first the Kingdom of God and his righteousness, and all these things [i.e. the necessary material requirements of life] will be added unto you.' We are so used to giving most of our time to material pursuits that we dare not neglect them for a moment. It need hardly be said that our Lord's words do not invite idleness or laziness, but rather that when we have our priorities right our occupations fall into a proper order. And further, the necessary material requirements are not ignored but, instead of their drawing us away from God, they are now sacramental of our life of citizenship in God's Kingdom. The Gospel of the Incarnation is not a denial of the material. On the contrary, it recognizes the importance of the material when it is seen as the means whereby we can live triumphantly in God's Kingdom, and when it is used to hasten that Kingdom which in Christ has already come.

If there is any conflict between our occupation with the material and our duty to God, the choice is clear. Our material possessions must never be allowed to come between us and God; but if all that we have and are is yielded to Him for His glory and His service then,

having lived as faithful stewards, we shall one
day be gladdened by the word of welcome:
'Well done, good and faithful servant.'

But all this is much easier to write or to
read than to live. The emphasis falls heavily on
the word *first*. This must never be forgotten
for nothing must be allowed to weaken our
Lord's total demand upon us. Nothing matters
but our fellowship with Him and our life of
discipleship. His Will and His Kingdom must
come first absolutely, all the time; and in
childlike faith we must trust Him to provide
for us as He sees fit. And if we are sometimes
tempted to doubt, surely the invincible gaiety
and power of a penniless Francis of Assisi
for ever demonstrates that 'a man's life con-
sisteth not in the abundance of the things
which he possesseth' but of his being rich
towards God.

So we are bidden to seek the Kingdom of
God first. But what do we mean by the Kingdom of God? It is perfectly correct to think
of it within the context of our personal lives
and our personal obedience. For us it signi-

fies a resolve to live our lives according to God's Will. We pray that as with the first disciples, so with us—people will 'take knowledge of us that we have been with Jesus', that somehow, by His grace, our lives will reflect His spirit, His love and His service. In this individual realm we should all the time be changing into the likeness of Christ.

More, however, is included in this phrase, 'The Kingdom of God'. It includes our loyalty to the Church as an outpost of Christ's Kingdom. It is not the Kingdom but it is the agency by which it is established, and therefore the Church should reveal in its corporate life the reality of the Kingdom. In this world of space and time the Church has to engage in administrative and organizational activity of all kinds, and it is important that this work should be done as efficiently as possible. But when we talk about seeking the Kingdom, we mean rather our identification with the witnessing and worshipping community of the Church as a whole and our local church in particular. By the quality of our living, corporately and individually, we should make the church a visible embodiment of the Kingdom. It should be the kind of community in which self-seeking is outlawed, in which self-assertiveness is forgotten, in which selfishness in any form is exiled. It should be a little bit of the world that has worked out the meaning of its redemption and which thus restores humanity to the purpose of its original creation. It will demand prayer and sacrifice, generosity and compassion, and much more besides—but we cannot be said to be seeking the Kingdom first unless we are giving ourselves humbly in Christ's service in the fellowship of His Church.

There is still one further field of responsibility. As our Lord ascended up into heaven He commissioned His disciples with these words: 'All power is given unto me in heaven and in earth. Go ye therefore, and teach all nations, baptizing them in the Name of the Father, and of the Son, and of the Holy Ghost; teaching them to observe all things whatsoever I have commanded you: and lo, I am with you alway, even unto the end of the world.' (St. Matthew 28: 18-20) The Gospel of the Kingdom which Christ proclaimed is destined to have its impact on national and international life. It is the Christian's duty to work for the coming of the Kingdom and, in so doing, to create a social order which approximates to that society which Christ described in His Sermon on the Mount.

Alas, the Christian knows only too well the vast gulf that divides the ideal from the reality but, in so far as he has influence, he has to press for the application of Christian principles to civic and social existence. He has to make his political decisions in the light of his faith. He has to make his economic and industrial decisions as a Christian seeking to do God's will.

He is not so foolish as to believe that the Kingdom of God can be established by secular methods, nor is he so foolish as to believe that his working life, his political life, his financial life, are of no concern to God. It is often anything but easy for the Christian to know how

he should act in the complexities of a twen-
tieth-century situation, but this is no excuse
for abdication. Its very difficulty makes greater
demands upon him; he must try to weigh up
the *pros* and *cons* not for his own advantage
but as a Christian living as a citizen of Christ's
Kingdom. And as a Christian, he must work
to implement those policies which further
Christ's cause and to hinder those that mili-
tate against it.

The discomfort of the Christian life rests
largely in its all-inclusiveness. If religion were
but one compartment of our lives and the
remainder at our personal disposal, it would all
be much less costly for us. But this is not so.
Because God became man in Jesus Christ, all
life is the sphere of our obedience and in all
life we have to seek first the Kingdom of God.

In fact all the *Uncomfortable Words* that we
have considered in these chapters could be
embraced by this demand to put God and
His will first in everything. Yet it is those
who willingly and unreservedly abandon themselves to God who find a return far greater

than anything they have surrendered, and who would not exchange their Faith however demanding for all the prosperity and popularity in the world.

'He that spared not his own Son but delivered him up for us all, how shall he not with him freely give us all things.'

'Thanks be to God for his unspeakable gift.'